Arts Magnet Colle

Designs by Conn Baker Gibney

Size: Individual stitched motifs vary from approximately 2¾ inches W x 3⅞ inches H (7cm x 9.8cm) to 2½ inches W x 6⅜ inches H (6.4cm x 16.2cm), excluding embellishments

Skill Level: Beginner

Materials

Each Magnet
- ❏ Small piece of 7-count plastic canvas
- ❏ Red Heart Classic Art. E267 medium weight yarn as listed in color key
- ❏ Round button magnet or small strip magnet
- ❏ Hot-glue gun

Ballet Slippers
- ❏ 1 yard (1m) ¼-inch (7mm) pink satin ribbon

Chef's Hat
- ❏ #3 pearl cotton as listed in color key

Comedy & Tragedy
- ❏ #3 pearl cotton as listed in color key
- ❏ 2 (½-inch/12mm) light pink pompoms
- ❏ 30 inches (0.8m) ⅛-inch (3mm) bright pink satin ribbon
- ❏ 5mm faceted round crystal

Director's Slate
- ❏ 2½-inch (6.4cm) silver star appliqué

Viola
- ❏ #3 pearl cotton as listed in color key
- ❏ Toothpick

Palette
- ❏ 4¼-inch (10.8cm) makeup brush
- ❏ Green craft paint

Quill
- ❏ Rainbow Gallery Plastic Canvas 7 metallic needlepoint yarn as listed in color key
- ❏ Metallic gold craft paint
- ❏ Toothpick

Stage Bill
- ❏ Rainbow Gallery Plastic Canvas 7 metallic needlepoint yarn as listed in color key
- ❏ #3 pearl cotton as listed in color key

Treble Clef
- ❏ #3 pearl cotton as listed in color key

Project Note

Refer to photos throughout for assembly.

Stitching Step by Step

Ballet Slippers

1 Cut circle, slipper A and slipper B from plastic canvas according to graphs (page 5).

2 Stitch plastic canvas according to graphs, filling in uncoded areas with grenadine Continental Stitches. Overcast edges according to graphs.

3 Referring to stitch diagram, work Turkey Loop Stitches on slippers with grenadine yarn where indicated by blue dots on graph.

4 Thread two 4½-inch (11.4cm) pieces of ribbon through slipper B from back to front where indicated by red dots on graph until ½-inch (1.3cm) ends remain on reverse side; glue tails to reverse side of slipper. Thread a 6-inch (15.2cm) piece of ribbon through slipper A where indicated by red dot on graph, centering slipper on ribbon.

5 Arrange slippers and ribbon ties, adjusting positions of slippers and length of ribbons as desired. Trim ribbon ends as needed and glue to front of stitched plastic canvas circle.

6 Tie two or three bows from remaining ribbon; center and glue to plastic canvas circle, concealing ribbon ends.

7 Glue magnet to reverse side of circle.

Chef's Hat

1 Cut hat from plastic canvas according to graph (page 3).

2 Stitch plastic canvas according to graph, filling in uncoded areas with white Continental Stitches. Overcast edges according to graph.

3 Straight Stitch lettering using red #3 pearl cotton.

4 Glue magnet to reverse side.

Comedy & Tragedy

1 Cut masks from plastic canvas according to graphs (page 3).

2 Stitch plastic canvas and Overcast edges according to graphs.

3 Straight Stitch eye lines and eyebrows using black #3 pearl cotton.

4 Cut ribbon into four equal pieces; curl ribbons over a flat edge. Glue one end of each to reverse side of mask in top corner.

5 Glue pink pompoms to masks where indicated by blue dots on graphs. Glue crystal to tragedy mask where indicated by red dot.

6 Glue magnet to reverse side of each mask.

Director's Slate

1 Cut slate bottom and top from plastic canvas according to graphs (page 5).

2 Stitch plastic canvas according to graphs, filling in uncoded areas with black Continental Stitches. Overcast edges according to graphs, working Overcast stitches in the same direction as adjacent center stitches.

3 Glue star to slate bottom where indicated by red dot on graph. Glue lower left edge of slate top behind upper left edge of slate bottom.

4 Glue magnet to reverse side of slate bottom.

Viola

1 Cut plastic canvas according to graph (page 4).

2 Stitch plastic canvas and Overcast edges according to graph.

3 Work black yarn French Knots, black #3 pearl cotton French Knots and black #3 pearl cotton Straight Stitches according to graph, wrapping fiber once around needle for French Knots. Work ecru #3 pearl cotton Straight Stitches, then black yarn Straight Stitches.

4 Glue toothpick to reverse side of neck for additional support. Glue magnet to reverse side of viola.

Palette

1 Cut plastic canvas according to graph (page 3), cutting away gray area.

2 Stitch plastic canvas according to graph, filling in uncoded areas with warm brown Continental Stitches. Overcast edges according to graph.

3 Dip bristles of makeup brush into green paint; let dry. Insert brush handle through hole in palette as shown; secure with hot glue.

4 Glue magnet to reverse side.

Quill

1 Cut plastic canvas according to graph (page 4).

2 Stitch plastic canvas and Overcast edges according to graph.

3 Dip ½ inch (1.3cm) at one end of toothpick into gold paint; let dry. Glue toothpick to reverse side of plastic canvas, allowing painted tip to show at end of quill.

4 Glue magnet to reverse side.

Stage Bill

1 Cut plastic canvas according to graph (page 4).

2 Stitch plastic canvas according to graph, filling in uncoded areas with jockey red Continental Stitches. Overcast edges according to graph.

3 Backstitch and Straight Stitch lettering using black #3 pearl cotton. Straight Stitch crown and work French Knot using gold metallic yarn, and wrapping yarn once around needle for French Knot.

4 Glue magnet to reverse side.

Treble Clef

1 Cut plastic canvas according to graph (page 5).

2 Stitch plastic canvas according to graph, filling in uncoded areas with white Continental Stitches. Overcast edges according to graph.

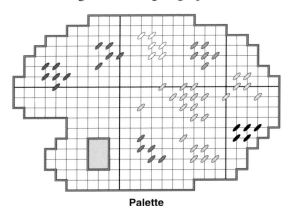

Palette
25 holes x 17 holes
Cut 1, cutting away gray area

COLOR KEY
PALETTE

Yards	Medium Weight Yarn
1 (1m)	☐ White #1
1 (1m)	■ Black #12
1 (1m)	☐ Yellow #230
1 (1m)	☐ Medium coral #252
1 (1m)	☐ Medium teal #359
1 (1m)	☐ Light lavender #579
1 (1m)	■ Amethyst #588
1 (1m)	☐ Skipper blue #848
1 (1m)	☐ Jockey red #902
4 (3.7m)	Uncoded areas are warm brown #336 Continental Stitches
	╱ Warm brown #336 Overcast

Color numbers given are for Red Heart Classic Art. E267 medium weight yarn.

3 Straight Stitch staff lines using black #3 pearl cotton.

4 Glue magnet to reverse side.

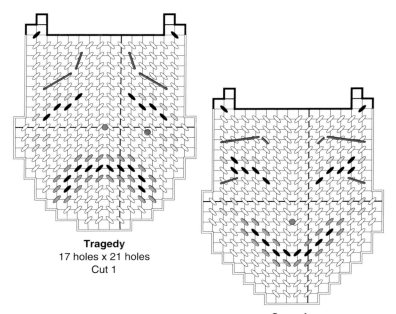

Tragedy
17 holes x 21 holes
Cut 1

Comedy
17 holes x 21 holes
Cut 1

COLOR KEY
COMEDY & TRAGEDY

Yards	Medium Weight Yarn
7 (6.5m)	☐ White #1
2 (1.9m)	■ Black #12
1 (1m)	☐ Sea coral #246
1 (1m)	☐ Mist green #681
1 (1m)	☐ Grenadine #730
	#3 Pearl Cotton
1 (1m)	╱ Black #310 Straight Stitch
	● Attach pompom
	● Attach crystal

Color numbers given are for Red Heart Classic Art. E267 medium weight yarn and DMC #3 pearl cotton.

COLOR KEY
CHEF'S HAT

Yards	Medium Weight Yarn
2 (1.9m)	☐ Light periwinkle #827
3 (2.8m)	Uncoded areas are white #1 Continental Stitches
	#3 Pearl Cotton
1 (1m)	╱ Red #321 Straight Stitch

Color numbers given are for Red Heart Classic Art. E267 medium weight yarn and DMC #3 pearl cotton.

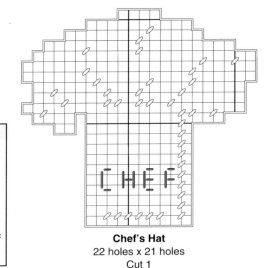

Chef's Hat
22 holes x 21 holes
Cut 1

Stage Bill
17 holes x 23 holes
Cut 1

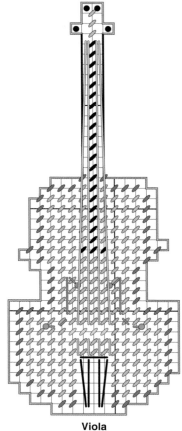

Viola
16 holes x 40 holes
Cut 1

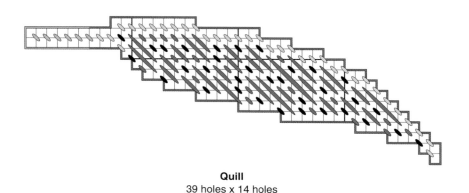

Quill
39 holes x 14 holes
Cut 1

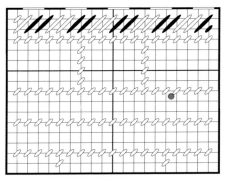

Slate Bottom
20 holes x 16 holes
Cut 1

Slate Top
20 holes x 3 holes
Cut 1

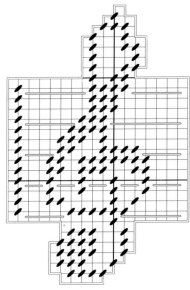

Treble Clef
17 holes x 27 holes
Cut 1

COLOR KEY
DIRECTOR'S SLATE
Yards	Medium Weight Yarn
3 (2.8m)	☐ White #1
5 (4.6m)	■ Black #12
	Uncoded areas are black #12 Continental Stitches
	● Attach star appliqué

Color numbers given are for Red Heart Classic Art. E267 medium weight yarn.

COLOR KEY
TREBLE CLEF
Yards	Medium Weight Yarn
2 (1.9m)	■ Black #12
4 (3.7m)	Uncoded areas are white #1 Continental Stitches
	⁄ White #1 Overcast
	#3 Pearl Cotton
1 (1m)	⁄ Black #310 Backstitch and Straight Stitch

Color numbers given are for Red Heart Classic Art. E267 medium weight yarn and DMC #3 pearl cotton.

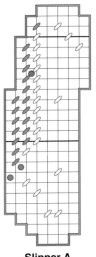

Slipper A
8 holes x 23 holes
Cut 1

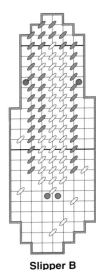

Slipper B
8 holes x 23 holes
Cut 1

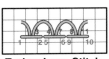

Turkey Loop Stitch

Circle
5 holes x 5 holes
Cut 1

COLOR KEY
BALLET SLIPPERS
Yards	Medium Weight Yarn
1 (1m)	☐ Pale rose #755
2 (1.9m)	▨ New berry #760
4 (3.7m)	Uncoded areas are grenadine #730 Continental Stitches
	⁄ Grenadine #730 Overcast
	● Grenadine #730 Turkey Loop Stitch
	● Attach ribbon

Color numbers given are for Red Heart Classic Art. E267 medium weight yarn.

"God Bless" Card

Design by Alida Macor

Size: **Stitched motif:** 4¼ inches W x 3 inches H
(10.8cm x 7.6cm)

Completed card: 5½ inches W x
3¼ inches H (14cm x 8.2cm)

Skill Level: Beginner

Materials

❑ ⅓ sheet 10-count plastic canvas
❑ DMC #3 pearl cotton as listed in color key
❑ 5½ x 3¼-inch (14cm x 8.2cm) trifold needlework card with 3½ x 2½-inch (8.9cm x 6.5cm) heart-shaped opening from Yarn Tree Designs
❑ Matching envelope
❑ #16 tapestry needle
❑ Craft glue or glue stick

Stitching Step by Step

1 Cut plastic canvas according to graph.

2 Stitch plastic canvas according to graph. Overcast edges with very light peach.

3 Glue stitched plastic canvas in card, centering stitched design behind opening.

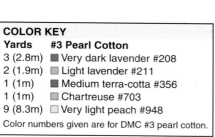

COLOR KEY

Yards	#3 Pearl Cotton
3 (2.8m)	■ Very dark lavender #208
2 (1.9m)	▨ Light lavender #211
1 (1m)	■ Medium terra-cotta #356
1 (1m)	▨ Chartreuse #703
9 (8.3m)	☐ Very light peach #948

Color numbers given are for DMC #3 pearl cotton.

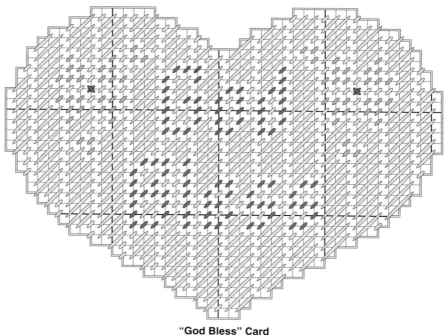

"God Bless" Card
41 holes x 30 holes
Cut 1

Butterflies & Blooms Magnet

Design by Nancy Barrett

Size: **Trellis:** 8¾ inches W x 7 inches H
(22.2cm x 17.8cm)
Flower magnets: 2 inches W x 1¾ inches H
(5.1cm x 4.4cm)
Skill Level: Beginner

Materials

❏ 1 sheet 10-count plastic canvas
❏ Medium weight yarn as listed in color key
❏ #16 tapestry needle
❏ Adhesive-backed magnet strips

Project Note

Work all stitches using 2 plies separated from a length of yarn unless instructed otherwise.

Stitching Step by Step

Trellis

1 Cut left, center and right uprights, and top, middle and bottom crosspieces from plastic canvas according to graphs (pages 8 and 9).

2 Stitch plastic canvas according to graphs, Overcasting edges as you stitch.

3 Referring to assembly diagram throughout, arrange trellis pieces. Tack layers together at intersections using white yarn.

Flowers & Butterflies

1 Cut two butterflies, 12 small petals, 24 large petals and 18 leaves from plastic canvas according to graphs (page 9).

2 Stitch butterflies according to graph, Overcasting edges as you stitch. Straight Stitch bodies using full strand of black yarn, carrying stitches over the edges to reverse side.

3 Stitch leaves according to graph, Overcasting edges as you stitch.

4 Stitch eight small petals according to graph, Overcasting edges as you stitch. Stitch remaining small petals replacing bright purple with rose.

5 Stitch 12 large petals according to graph, Overcasting edges as you stitch. Stitch remaining large petals replacing bright purple with rose.

6 *Assemble small flowers:* Arrange small petals in groups of four of matching colors with tips touching in center. Join petals of each flower with Straight Stitches across center, using light lavender yarn to join rose petals and light pink yarn to join bright purple petals.

7 *Assemble large flowers:* Arrange and join large petals as for small flowers. Arrange three leaves between petals on reverse side of each flower, tacking petals and leaves together.

Assembly

1 Referring to photo throughout, tack butterflies and flowers to trellis as desired, reserving a few large flowers and/or butterflies for individual magnets, if desired.

2 Affix magnet strips to reverse side of trellis and reserved flowers and/or butterflies.

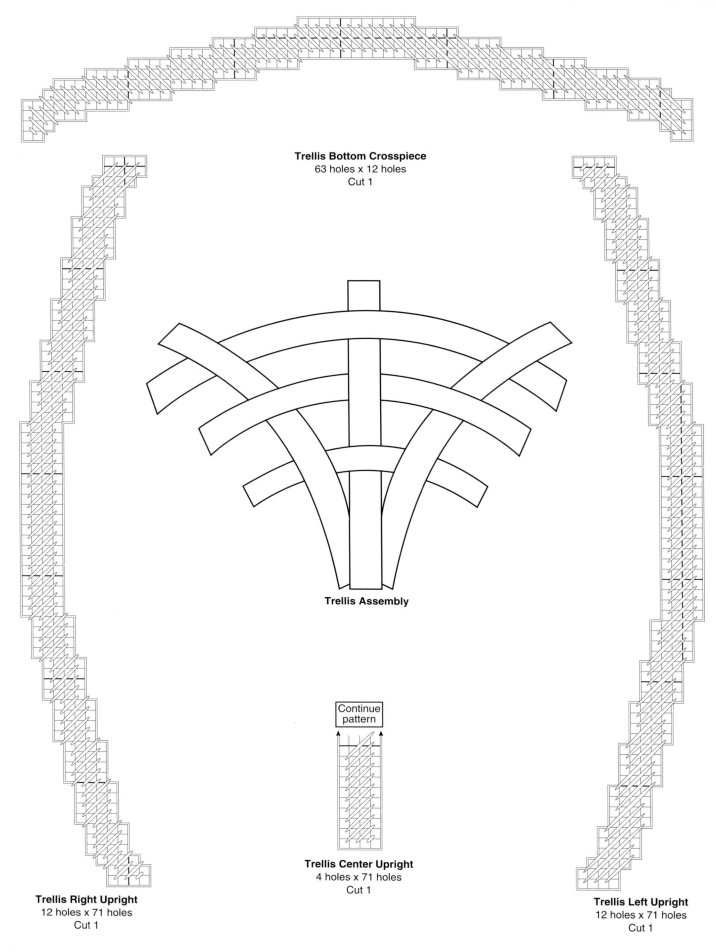

Trellis Bottom Crosspiece
63 holes x 12 holes
Cut 1

Trellis Assembly

Continue
pattern

Trellis Center Upright
4 holes x 71 holes
Cut 1

Trellis Right Upright
12 holes x 71 holes
Cut 1

Trellis Left Upright
12 holes x 71 holes
Cut 1

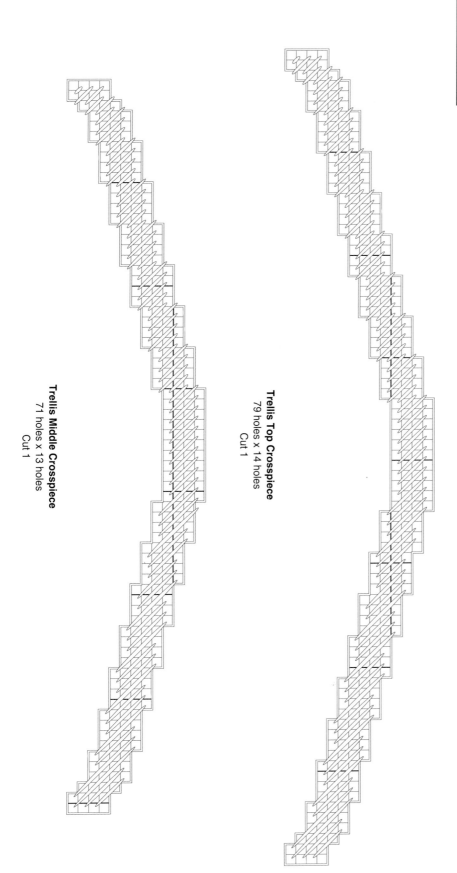

Trellis Middle Crosspiece
71 holes x 13 holes
Cut 1

Trellis Top Crosspiece
79 holes x 14 holes
Cut 1

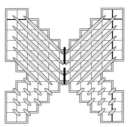

Trellis Butterfly
11 holes x 11 holes
Cut 2

Trellis Leaf
5 holes x 9 holes
Cut 18

Trellis Small Petal
3 holes x 3 holes
Cut 12
Stitch 8 as graphed
Stitch 4, replacing bright
purple with rose

Trellis Large Petal
5 holes x 7 holes
Cut 24
Stitch 12 as graphed
Stitch 12, replacing bright
purple with rose

Clip-on Tie Bookmark

Design by Ronda Bryce

Size: 2¾ inches W x 6¼ inches H (7cm x 15.9cm)
Skill Level: Beginner

Materials

- ❑ Small piece 7-count plastic canvas
- ❑ Uniek Needloft plastic canvas yarn as listed in color key
- ❑ 2-inch (5.1cm) paper clip
- ❑ Sewing needle and navy blue thread
- ❑ #16 tapestry needle

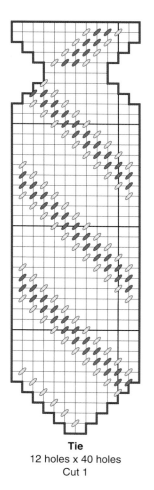

Tie
12 holes x 40 holes
Cut 1

Stitching Step by Step

1 Cut plastic canvas according to graph.

2 Stitch plastic canvas according to graph; Overcast with dark royal.

3 Using sewing needle and navy blue thread, stitch paper clip to reverse side of plastic canvas near top edge so that tie can be used as a clip-on bookmark.

COLOR KEY	
Yards	**Plastic Canvas Yarn**
2 (1.9m)	■ Christmas red #02
2 (1.9m)	☐ Yellow #57
7 (6.5m)	Uncoded areas are dark royal #48 Continental Stitches
	╱ Dark royal #48 Overcast
Color numbers given are for Uniek Needloft plastic canvas yarn.	

Garden Fridgies

Designs by Mary T. Cosgrove

Size: Individual stitched motifs vary from approximately 1¾ inches W x 3 inches H (4.4cm x 7.6cm) to 3 inches W x 3 inches H (7.6cm x 7.6cm)

Skill Level: Beginner

Materials

One Set

❑ ½ sheet 7-count plastic canvas
❑ Uniek Needloft plastic canvas yarn as listed in color keys
❑ 5 (½-inch/1.3cm) magnet strips
❑ #16 tapestry needle
❑ Hot-glue gun

Stitching Step by Step

1 Cut plastic canvas according to graphs (page 12).

2 Stitch plastic canvas according to graphs, filling in uncoded areas with Continental Stitches of the following colors: strawberry—red; broccoli—fern; watermelon—watermelon; corn—lemon; carrot—bright orange. Overcast according to graphs.

3 When background stitching is complete, work embroidery stitches:

Strawberry—Straight Stitch mouth and nose with white; Straight Stitch seeds with bright green; Backstitch eyes with black.

Broccoli—Work French Knots with bright green, wrapping yarn once around needle. Straight Stitch mouth and nose with white; Backstitch eyes with black; work Straight Stitches among French Knots with holly.

Watermelon—Straight Stitch nose with white; Backstitch eyes and Straight Stitch mouth with black; Backstitch rind with holly.

Corn—Backstitch eyes and Straight Stitch mouth with black; Backstitch tips of husk with fern.

Carrot—Backstitch eyes and Straight Stitch mouth with black.

4 Hot-glue a magnet to the reverse side of each stitched plastic canvas piece.

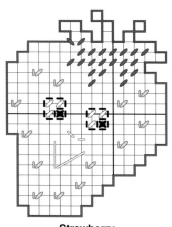

Strawberry
15 holes x 20 holes
Cut 1

COLOR KEY
STRAWBERRY

Yards	Plastic Canvas Yarn
1 (1m)	■ Black #00
1 (1m)	■ Christmas green #28
1 (1m)	□ White #41
1 (1m)	■ Bright green #61
3 (2.8m)	Uncoded area is red #01 Continental Stitches
	╱ Red #01 Overcast
	╱ Black #00 Backstitch
	╱ White #41 Straight Stitch
	╱ Bright green #61 Straight Stitch

Color numbers given are for Uniek Needloft plastic canvas yarn.

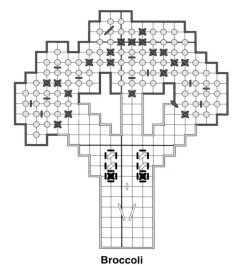

Broccoli
20 holes x 23 holes
Cut 1

COLOR KEY
BROCCOLI

Yards	Plastic Canvas Yarn
1 (1m)	■ Black #00
3 (2.8m)	■ Holly #27
1 (1m)	□ White #41
2 (1.9m)	Uncoded areas are fern #23 Continental Stitches
	╱ Fern #23 Overcast
	╱ Black #00 Backstitch
	╱ Holly #27 Straight Stitch
	╱ White #41 Straight Stitch
3 (2.8m)	○ Bright green #61 French Knot

Color numbers given are for Uniek Needloft plastic canvas yarn.

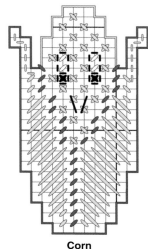

Corn
13 holes x 22 holes
Cut 1

COLOR KEY
CORN

Yards	Plastic Canvas Yarn
1 (1m)	■ Black #00
2 (1.9m)	□ Fern #23
2 (1.9m)	■ Holly #27
1 (1m)	□ White #41
1 (1m)	□ Yellow #57
1 (1m)	Uncoded areas are lemon #20 Continental Stitches
	╱ Black #00 Backstitch and Straight Stitch
	╱ Fern #23 Backstitch

Color numbers given are for Uniek Needloft plastic canvas yarn.

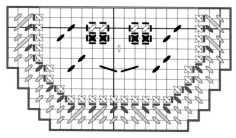

Watermelon
21 holes x 12 holes
Cut 1

COLOR KEY
WATERMELON

Yards	Plastic Canvas Yarn
1 (1m)	■ Black #00
1 (1m)	■ Moss #25
2 (1.9m)	■ Holly #27
2 (1.9m)	□ White #41
2 (1.9m)	Uncoded area is watermelon #55 Continental Stitches
	╱ Watermelon #55 Overcast
	╱ Black #00 Backstitch and Straight Stitch
	╱ Holly #27 Backstitch
	╱ White #41 Straight Stitch

Color numbers given are for Uniek Needloft plastic canvas yarn.

COLOR KEY
CARROT

Yards	Plastic Canvas Yarn
1 (1m)	■ Black #00
1 (1m)	□ Fern #23
1 (1m)	■ Christmas green #28
1 (1m)	□ White #41
2 (1.9m)	Uncoded area is bright orange #58 Continental Stitches
	╱ Bright orange #58 Overcast
	╱ Black #00 Backstitch and Straight Stitch

Color numbers given are for Uniek Needloft plastic canvas yarn.

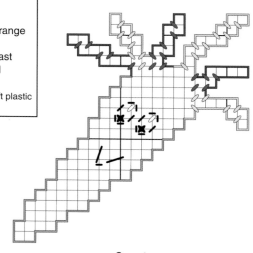

Carrot
22 holes x 22 holes
Cut 1

Take-Along Hopscotch

Design by Mary T. Cosgrove

Size: **Hopscotch Board:** 6⅞ inches W x
13⅝ inches H (17.5cm x 34.6cm)
Numbers Wheel: 4⅝ inches square (11.8cm)
Player: 2 inches W x 3¼ inches H x
1¼ inches D (5.1cm x 8.2cm 3.2cm)
Marker: 1 inch square (2.5cm)
Skill Level: Beginner

Materials

- ❑ 1 sheet 7-count plastic canvas
- ❑ Uniek Needloft plastic canvas yarn as listed in
  color key
- ❑ Clear thread
- ❑ White pony bead
- ❑ Size 3/0 (¼-inch/7mm) sew-on snap
- ❑ #16 tapestry needle
- ❑ Clear-drying craft glue

Stitching Step by Step

1 Cut hopscotch board, numbers wheel, two spinners, two players, four stands and four markers from plastic canvas according to graphs (below and page 14).

2 Stitch hopscotch board, numbers wheel and one spinner according to graphs, filling in uncoded areas on hopscotch board with black Continental Stitches. One spinner will remain unstitched.

3 Stitch one player, one stand and one marker according to graphs, filling in uncoded areas on player with pink Continental Stitches. Stitch second player, one stand and one marker substituting bright orange for bright blue. Remaining stands and markers will remain unstitched.

4 *Work embroidery stitches:* Using black yarn throughout, Straight Stitch numerals on numbers wheel. Backstitch nose and mouth on players; work French Knot eyes on players, wrapping yarn once around needle.

5 Overcast hopscotch board and numbers wheel with white. Holding unstitched spinner against reverse side of stitched spinner, Whipstitch pieces together with black.

6 Overcast edges of players *except bottoms of feet* according to graphs. Using yarn to match dress color, thread yarn through heads where indicated by yellow dots on graph. Tie yarn in tiny hair bows; trim ends. Apply a tiny amount of glue to cut ends to prevent fraying.

7 Using pink yarn and stitching through each pair of holes twice, Whipstitch bottoms of players' feet to matching stitched stand where indicated by red lines on graph. Whipstitch unstitched stands to bottom using matching yarn.

8 Whipstitch unstitched markers to stitched markers using matching yarn.

Spinner Assembly

1 Using clear thread throughout, stitch pony bead to center of numbers wheel with half of sew-on snap on top of bead.

2 Stitch remaining half of snap to underside of spinner where indicated by purple dot on graph. Snap spinner onto wheel.

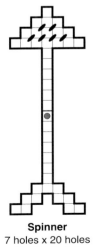

Spinner
7 holes x 20 holes
Cut 2, stitch 1

COLOR KEY

Yards	Plastic Canvas Yarn
30 (27.5m)	■ Black #00
2 (1.9m)	■ Maple #13
14 (12.9m)	☐ White #41
9 (8.3m)	■ Bright orange #58
8 (7.4m)	■ Bright blue #60
	Uncoded areas on hopscotch board are black #00 Continental Stitches
4 (3.7m)	Uncoded areas on player are pink #07 Contintental Stitches
	∕ Pink #07 Overcast
	✓ Black #00 Backstitch and Straight Stitch
	● Black #00 (1-wrap) French Knot
	○ Attach pigtail tie
	● Attach snap

Color numbers given are for Uniek Needloft plastic canvas yarn.

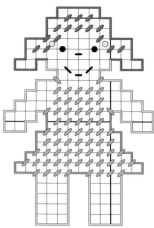

Player
14 holes x 21 holes
Cut 2
Stitch 1 as graphed
Stitch 1, replacing bright
blue with bright orange

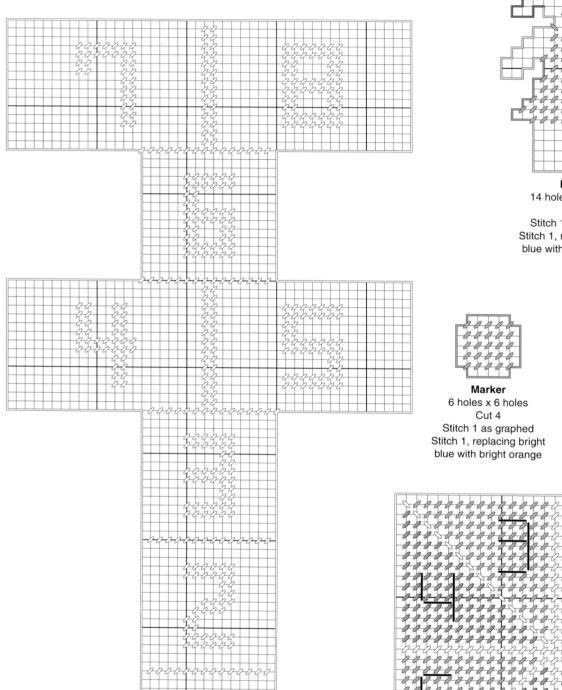

Marker
6 holes x 6 holes
Cut 4
Stitch 1 as graphed
Stitch 1, replacing bright
blue with bright orange

Stand
8 holes x 8 holes
Cut 4
Stitch 1 as graphed
Stitch 1, replacing bright
blue with bright orange

Hopscotch Board
45 holes x 90 holes
Cut 1

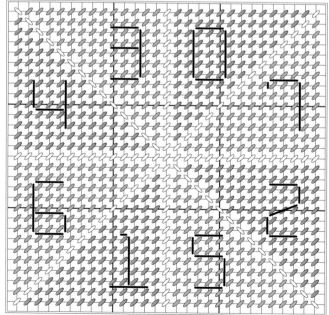

Numbers Wheel
30 holes x 30 holes
Cut 1

Gifts for the Bookworm

Potted Poinsettia

Design by Celia Lange Designs

Materials

- ¼ sheet 10-count plastic canvas
- DMC #3 pearl cotton as listed in color key
- ⅓ yard (0.4m) ⅝-inch-wide (15mm) green grosgrain ribbon
- #18 tapestry needle
- Hot-glue gun

Stitching Step by Step

1 Cut pot, saucer, rim, poinsettia center and two sets of poinsettia petals from 10-count plastic canvas according to graphs (page 17).

2 Stitch plastic canvas according to graphs, substituting garnet for red on one set of poinsettia petals.

3 Overcast pieces according to graphs.

4 *Work embroidery stitches:* Work red and yellow Backstitches on pot, carrying stitches over edges as shown. Work lemon French Knots on poinsettia center, wrapping pearl cotton once around needle.

5 Referring to photo throughout, glue red petals on top of garnet petals, alternating positions of petals evenly. Glue poinsettia center in center of flower. Center and glue rim to top edge and saucer to bottom edge of pot as shown.

6 Cut ribbon to desired length; glue a stitched motif to each end of ribbon.

Berry Best Friend

Design by Linda Wyszynski

Materials

- ¼ sheet ivory 14-count plastic canvas
- DMC 6-strand embroidery floss as listed in color key
- ¾ yard (0.7m) ⅝-inch-wide (15mm) red grosgrain ribbon
- Green sewing thread
- Decorative strawberry button
- #24 tapestry needle

Project Notes

All stitching is worked using 4 strands separated from lengths of 6-strand embroidery floss. Separate all strands from an 18-inch (0.5m) length of floss, then recombine 4 strands and thread onto needle without twisting. Keep floss smooth and flat as you stitch for even coverage.

Stitching Step by Step

1 Cut two pieces of 14-count plastic canvas according to graph (page 17).

2 Work Cross Stitches on one piece according to graph for front, noting that some portions remain unstitched. Back will remain unstitched.

3 Referring to photo throughout and using needle and green thread, stitch button to right edge of front where indicated by black dots on graph.

4 Tie a knot in each end of ribbon. Find center of ribbon; crisscross ribbon sides, leaving a loop at the top. Referring to photo throughout, sandwich ribbon between stitched plastic canvas front and unstitched back, leaving loop protruding from center top edge.

5 Hold unstitched back and stitched front together. Work dark rose Running Stitch through both layers of plastic canvas—and ribbon, where needed—except at area under button, where Running Stitch will be worked through bottom layer of plastic canvas only.

Friends Are Dear to the Heart

Design by Linda Wyszynski

Materials

- ❏ ¼ sheet ivory 14-count plastic canvas
- ❏ DMC 6-strand embroidery floss as listed in color key
- ❏ RibbonFloss braided rayon ribbon from YLI Corp. as listed in color key
- ❏ ⅝-inch-wide (15mm) grosgrain ribbon:
  - ½ yard (0.5m) red
  - ½ yard (0.5m) dark green
- ❏ Red sewing thread
- ❏ Decorative heart button
- ❏ #24 tapestry needle

Project Notes

All Cross Stitches *worked with embroidery floss* are worked using 4 strands separated from lengths of 6-strand embroidery floss. Separate all strands from an 18-inch (0.5m) length of floss, then recombine 4 strands and thread onto needle without twisting. Keep floss smooth and flat as you stitch for even coverage.

Running Stitches are worked using 2 strands embroidery floss, separated in the same manner as for Cross Stitches.

Stitching Step by Step

1 Cut two pieces of 14-count plastic canvas according to graph.

2 Using 4 strands embroidery floss or a full strand of rayon ribbon, work Cross Stitches on one piece according to graph for front, noting that some portions remain unstitched. Back will remain unstitched.

3 Tie a knot in each end of each grosgrain ribbon. Overlap ribbons, placing red on top. Referring to photo throughout, center and sandwich grosgrain ribbons between stitched plastic canvas front and unstitched back.

4 Hold unstitched back and stitched front together. Work Running Stitch through both layers of plastic canvas—and ribbon, where needed—using 2 strands of ecru floss according to graph.

5 Using needle and red thread, stitch button to center of overlapped ribbons 3 inches (7.6cm) from top knots.

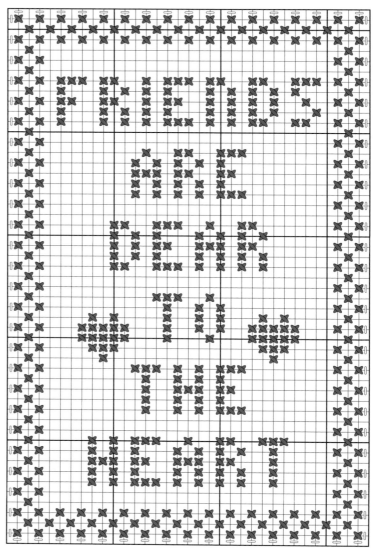

Friends Are Dear to the Heart
34 holes x 52 holes
Cut 2 from 14-count, stitch 1

COLOR KEY		
FRIENDS ARE DEAR TO THE HEART		
Yards	**6-Strand Embroidery Floss**	
6 (5.5m)	■	Very dark green #890 (4 strands)
2 (1.9m)	∕	Ecru (2-strand) Running Stitch
	Braided Rayon Ribbon	
4 (3.7m)	■	Red #142-012
Color numbers given are for DMC embroidery floss and Original RibbonFloss from YLI Corp.		

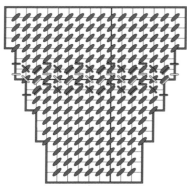

Potted Poinsettia Pot
17 holes x 17 holes
Cut 1 from 10-count

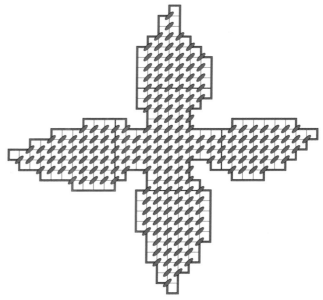

Potted Poinsettia Petals
29 holes x 28 holes
Cut 2 from 10-count
Stitch 1 as graphed
Stitch 1 replacing red with garnet

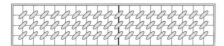

Potted Poinsettia Rim
19 holes x 4 holes
Cut 1 from 10-count

Potted Poinsettia Center
6 holes x 6 holes
Cut 1 from 10-count

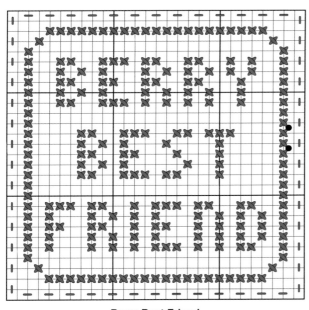

Berry Best Friend
28 holes x 28 holes
Cut 2 from 14-count, stitch 1

Potted Poinsettia Saucer
15 holes x 3 holes
Cut 1 from 10-count

COLOR KEY
BERRY BEST FRIEND

Yards	6-Strand Embroidery Floss
3 (2.8m)	■ Dark rose #326 (4 strands)
2 (1.9m)	■ Dark green #367 (4 strands)
	╱ Dark rose #326 (4-strand) Running Stitch
	● Attach button

Color numbers given are for DMC embroidery floss.

COLOR KEY
POTTED POINSETTIA

Yards	#3 Pearl Cotton
5 (4.6m)	■ Red #321
4 (3.7m)	■ Bright green #700
2 (1.9m)	☐ Yellow #725
4 (3.7m)	Garnet #815
	╱ Red #321 Backstitch
	╱ Yellow #725 Backstitch
1 (1m)	● Lemon #307 French Knot

Color numbers given are for DMC #3 pearl cotton.

Road Royalty Key Chains

Designs by Susan Leinberger

Size: 2¾ inches W x 3⅛ inches H (7cm x 7.9cm)
Skill Level: Beginner

Materials

Each Key Chain
- ❏ ½ sheet 7-count plastic canvas
- ❏ Uniek Needloft plastic canvas yarn as listed in color key
- ❏ Kreinik ⅛-inch Ribbon as listed in color key
- ❏ 32mm silver split key ring
- ❏ #16 tapestry needle
- ❏ Craft glue

Mom
- ❏ 6mm x 8mm faceted octagonal jewels #7460 from Westrim Crafts:
  - 2 red #8
  - 3 amethyst #612

Dad
- ❏ 6mm x 8mm faceted octagonal jewels #7460 from Westrim Crafts:
  - 2 aqua #18
  - 3 emerald #616

Stitching Step by Step

1 Cut front and back for desired design from plastic canvas according to graphs.

2 Stitch plastic canvas according to graphs, filling in uncoded areas with white Continental Stitches. Overcast cutouts with white.

3 Using ⅛-inch ribbon through step 5, when background stitching is complete, Backstitch lettering on back, using red for Mom key ring and royal blue for Dad key ring.

4 Straight Stitch top portion of crown on key ring front with gold, keeping ribbon smooth and flat. Backstitch around bottom portion of crown, using flame for Mom key ring and silver night for Dad key ring.

5 Backstitch lettering for "Mom" or "Dad" on key ring front using same color as for lettering on back.

6 Whipstitch front and back together with yarn, using red for Mom key ring and dark royal for Dad key ring.

7 Referring to photo, glue jewels across crown on front, alternating colors.

8 Thread split key ring through openings in top of stitched plastic canvas.

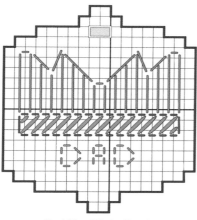

Dad Key Chain Front
18 holes x 20 holes
Cut 1, cutting away gray area

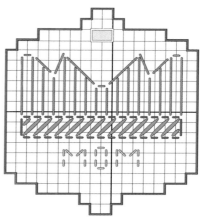

Mom Key Chain Front
18 holes x 20 holes
Cut 1, cutting away gray area

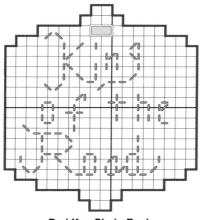

Dad Key Chain Back
18 holes x 20 holes
Cut 1, cutting away gray area

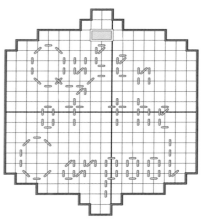

Mom Key Chain Back
18 holes x 20 holes
Cut 1, cutting away gray area

COLOR KEY
DAD

Yards	Plastic Canvas Yarn
9 (8.3m)	Uncoded areas are white #41 Continental Stitches
	⁄ White #41 Overcast
2 (1.9m)	⁄ Dark royal #48 Whipstitch
	1/8-Inch Ribbon
2 (1.9m)	■ Gold #002
	⁄ Gold #002 Straight Stitch
3 (2.8m)	⁄ Royal blue #033 Backstitch
1 (1m)	⁄ Silver night #393 Backstitch

Color numbers given are for Uniek Needloft plastic canvas yarn and Kreinik 1/8-inch Ribbon.

COLOR KEY
MOM

Yards	Plastic Canvas Yarn
9 (8.3m)	Uncoded areas are white #41 Continental Stitches
	⁄ White #41 Overcast
2 (1.9m)	⁄ Red #01 Whipstitch
	1/8-Inch Ribbon
2 (1.9m)	■ Gold #002
	⁄ Gold #002 Straight Stitch
3 (2.8m)	⁄ Red #003 Backstitch
1 (1m)	⁄ Flame #203 Backstitch

Color numbers given are for Uniek Needloft plastic canvas yarn and Kreinik 1/8-inch Ribbon.

Buggy Bag Clips

Designs by Nancy Marshall

Size: **Bee:** 3½ inches W x 5 inches H
(8.9cm x 12.7cm)
Ladybug: 3¼ inches W x 5 inches H
(8.2cm x 12.7cm)
Skill Level: Beginner

Materials

Each Bag Clip
- ❑ ¼ sheet 7-count plastic canvas
- ❑ Uniek Needloft plastic canvas yarn as listed in color key
- ❑ 1 inch (2.5cm) red 6-strand embroidery floss
- ❑ 2 (¼-inch/7mm) movable eyes
- ❑ Pompoms:
  2 (½-inch/12mm) black
  2 (³⁄₁₆-inch/5mm) pink
- ❑ 2 (1½-inch/3.8cm) pieces black chenille stem
- ❑ Spring-type clothespin
- ❑ #16 tapestry needle
- ❑ Clear-drying craft glue

Bee
- ❑ 3¼ x 4¼-inch piece (8.2cm x 10.8cm) white adhesive-backed Presto Felt from Kunin

Ladybug
- ❑ 3¼ x 4¼-inch piece (8.2cm x 10.8cm) red adhesive-backed Presto Felt from Kunin

Stitching Step by Step

1 Cut plastic canvas according to graph for desired project.

2 Using plastic canvas as a template, cut a matching piece from felt, trimming felt slightly smaller all around. Set felt aside for now.

3 Stitch plastic canvas according to graph, filling in uncoded areas on bee with white Continental Stitches and uncoded areas on ladybug with black Continental Stitches.

4 *Ladybug only:* Backstitch down center using black yarn.

5 Overcast according to graph.

6 Referring to photo and graph throughout, glue red floss to ladybug or bee over area marked with red line on graph. Glue pink pompoms at ends of smile; center and glue eyes above smile.

7 *Antennae:* Bend chenille stem pieces into shapes of antennae. Glue a black pompom to one end of each piece; glue other end to reverse side of bee or ladybug's head.

8 Peel backing from felt and press onto back of ladybug or bee, covering ends of antennae. Glue clothespin to felt at an angle.

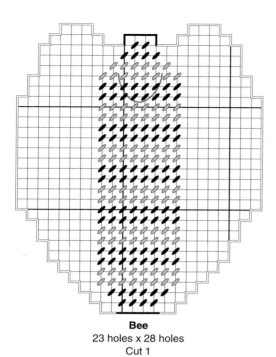

Bee
23 holes x 28 holes
Cut 1

COLOR KEY
BEE

Yards		Plastic Canvas Yarn
2 (1.9m)	■	Black #00
2 (1.9m)	▨	Tangerine #11
6 (5.5m)		Uncoded areas are white #41 Continental Stitches
	⟋	White #41 Overcast

Color numbers given are for Uniek Needloft plastic canvas yarn.

Ladybug
21 holes x 28 holes
Cut 1

COLOR KEY
LADYBUG

Yards		Plastic Canvas Yarn
3 (2.8m)	■	Christmas red #02 Uncoded areas are black #00 Continental Stitches
5 (4.6m)	⟋	Black #00 Backstitch and Overcast

Color numbers given are for Uniek Needloft plastic canvas yarn.

Towel Toppers

Designs by Jeannette Osborne

Size: **Towel Toppers A and B:** 7⅛ inches W x 5¾ inches H (18.1cm x 14.6cm), excluding towel
Towel Topper C: 6¾ inches W x 5¼ inches H (17.1cm x 13.3cm), excluding towel
Skill Level: Beginner

Materials

Each Towel Topper
❏ Uniek Needloft plastic canvas yarn as listed in color key
❏ Complementary kitchen towel
❏ 10 inches (25.4cm) white 1-inch (2.5cm) pregathered lace
❏ 7-inch (6.5cm) strip white ¾-inch (0.7cm) hook-and-loop tape
❏ Sewing machine, serger or pinking shears
❏ Sewing needle and complementary thread
❏ Straight pins (optional)
❏ #16 tapestry needle

Towel Topper A
❏ 1 sheet green 7-count plastic canvas
❏ ½-inch (13mm) red button
❏ 4 small white silk flowers with leaves
❏ Hot-glue gun

Towel Topper B
❏ 1 sheet teal 7-count plastic canvas
❏ 6-strand embroidery floss as listed in color key
❏ ½-inch (13mm) clear button

Towel Topper C
❏ 1 sheet light blue 7-count plastic canvas
❏ 6-strand embroidery floss as listed in color key
❏ ⅜-inch (10mm) white button

Stitching Step by Step

1 Cut plastic canvas according to graph for desired topper (page 23–25), cutting away gray shaded areas.

2 Stitch plastic canvas according to graph, noting that some areas remain unstitched. Overcast edges according to graph.

3 Add details to stitched toppers:

Topper A—Referring to photo, hot-glue silk flowers to area of fern stitching.

Toppers B and C—Straight Stitch flowers using red yarn. Straight Stitch flower stems and work Lazy Daisy leaves using 6 strands green embroidery floss.

Assembly

1 Cut towel in half crosswise. To prevent raveling, finish raw edge by machine stitching, serging or trimming with pinking shears.

2 Using sewing needle and complementary thread throughout, stitch button to topper where indicated by dot on graph.

3 Separate halves of hook-and-loop tape. Referring to Fig. 1 (page 25), sew lace and one half of hook-and-loop tape inside bottom edge of plastic canvas topper, sandwiching the lace between the plastic canvas and the smooth side of the hook-and-loop tape. Trim away excess hook-and-loop tape; turn under ends of lace and tack neatly in place.

4 Run a basting stitch across the cut edge of the towel; gather towel to fit across topper. Referring to Fig. 2 throughout, pin or baste remaining half of hook-and-loop tape along gathered edge on right side of towel; stitch in place. Remove pins or basting stitches.

5 Attach towel to underside of topper with hook-and-loop tape.

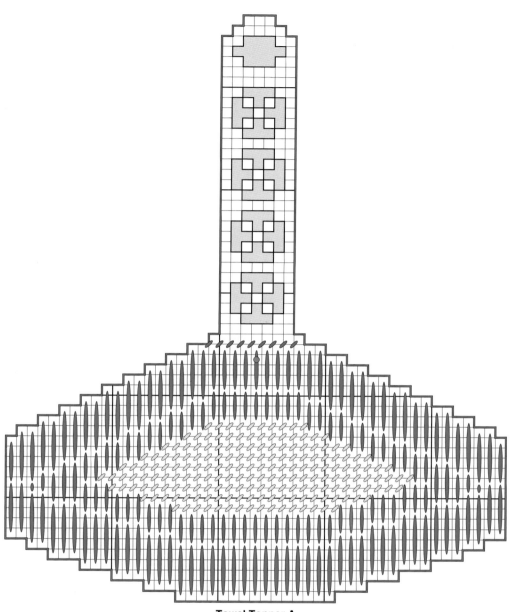

Towel Topper A
47 holes x 57 holes
Cut 1 from green,
cutting away gray areas

COLOR KEY
TOWEL TOPPER A

Yards	Plastic Canvas Yarn
6 (5.5m)	■ Red #01
4 (3.7m)	□ Fern #23
15 (13.8m)	■ Forest #29
	● Attach button

Color numbers given are for Uniek
Needloft plastic canvas yarn.

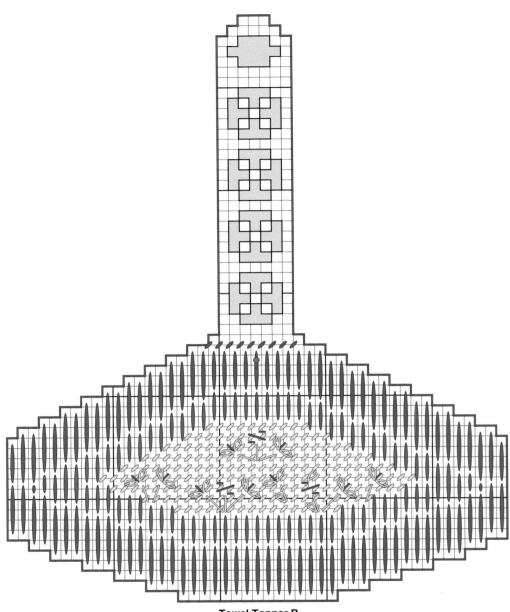

Towel Topper B
47 holes x 57 holes
Cut 1 from teal,
cutting away gray areas

COLOR KEY		
TOWEL TOPPER B		
Yards		**Plastic Canvas Yarn**
7 (6.4m)	■	Red #01
15 (13.8m)	■	Forest #29
4 (3.7m)	☐	Yellow #57
	╱	Red #01 Straight Stitch
6-Strand Embroidery Floss		
3 (2.8m)	╱	Green #910 (6-strand) Straight Stitch
	⬤	Green #910 (6-strand) Lazy Daisy Stitch
	●	Attach button

Color numbers given are for Uniek Needloft plastic canvas
yarn and DMC embroidery floss.

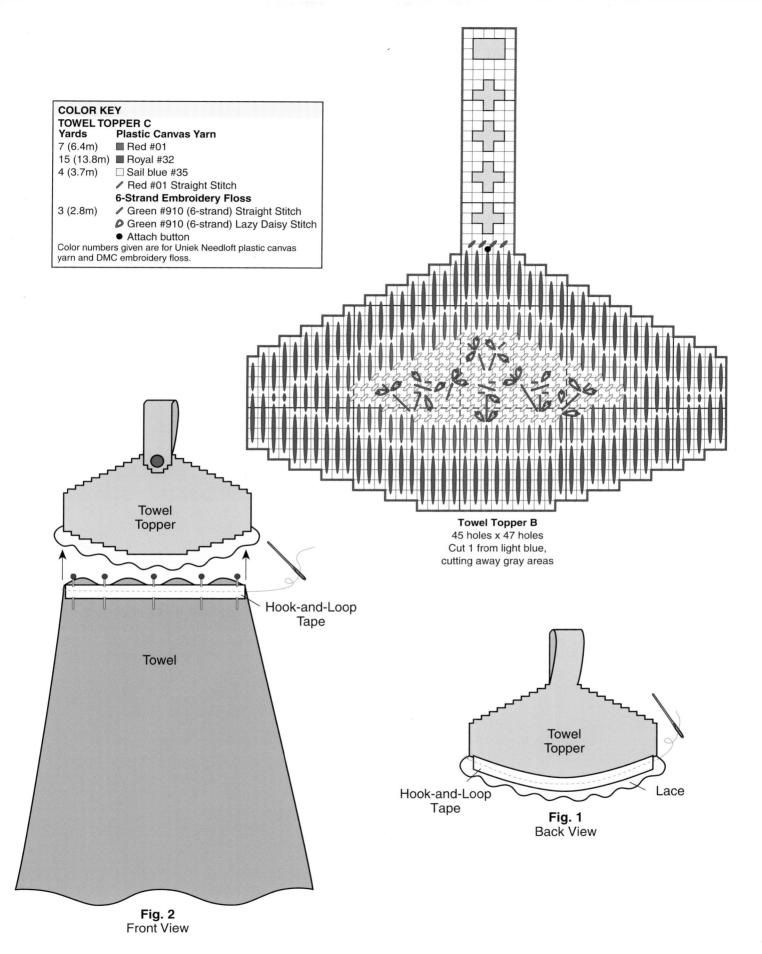

COLOR KEY
TOWEL TOPPER C

Yards	Plastic Canvas Yarn
7 (6.4m)	■ Red #01
15 (13.8m)	■ Royal #32
4 (3.7m)	□ Sail blue #35
	╱ Red #01 Straight Stitch

6-Strand Embroidery Floss

3 (2.8m)	╱ Green #910 (6-strand) Straight Stitch
	⟡ Green #910 (6-strand) Lazy Daisy Stitch
	● Attach button

Color numbers given are for Uniek Needloft plastic canvas yarn and DMC embroidery floss.

Towel Topper B
45 holes x 47 holes
Cut 1 from light blue,
cutting away gray areas

Towel Topper

Hook-and-Loop Tape

Towel

Fig. 2
Front View

Towel Topper

Hook-and-Loop Tape

Lace

Fig. 1
Back View

Little Animals Treat Holders

Designs by Christina Laws

Size: **Dog:** 3⅜ inches W x 6⅛ inches H
(8.6cm x 15.6cm)
Cat: 2⅜ inches W x 6⅜ inches H
(6cm x 16.2cm)
Mouse: 3⅛ inches W x 6¼ inches H
(7.9cm x 15.9cm)
Bear: 2½ inches W x 5¼ inches H
(6.4cm x 13.3cm)
Frog: 2 inches W x 4¾ inches H
(5.1cm x 12.1cm)
Skill Level: Beginner

Materials

Each Treat Holder
❑ ¼ sheet 7-count plastic canvas
❑ Medium weight yarn as listed in color key
❑ 2 (5mm) round black cabochons
❑ #16 tapestry needle
❑ Hot-glue gun

Project Note

The cat, dog, mouse and bear treat holders all use the same graph for the feet. A separate graph is presented for feet for the frog treat holder.

Stitching Step by Step

1 Cut two bodies and four feet for desired project from plastic canvas according to graphs (pages 27 and 28).

2 Stitch body front according to graph. Reverse back before stitching for cat, dog and mouse, and fill in backs completely with *Reverse Continental Stitches* worked in the main body color: gold for cat, pale yellow for dog, gray for mouse, brown for bear and green for frog.

3 *Work embroidery stitches:* Using black yarn throughout, Straight Stitch mouths on cat, dog, mouse and bear. Using red yarn, backstitch frog's mouth.

4 Stitch feet according to graphs, using the main body color, and Overcasting top, side and bottom edges outside arrows as you stitch.

5 Whipstitch front and back together according to graphs, Whipstitching short, straight edges of feet to body between arrows, working through all three layers. Whipstitch edges of feet together where they meet in center of treat holder.

6 Glue cabochons to treat holder for eyes where indicated by black dots on graphs.

7 Tuck treat inside treat holder's feet.

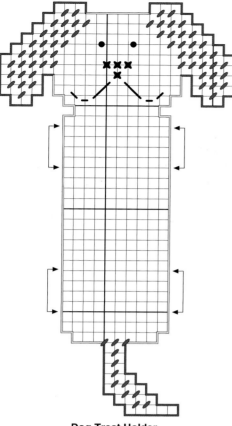

Dog Treat Holder
22 holes x 40 holes
Cut 2
Stitch front as graphed
Reverse back and stitch with
Reverse Continental Stitches,
omitting face

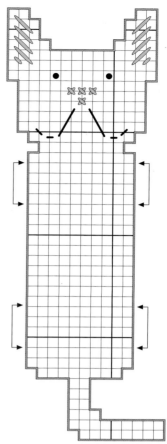

Cat Treat Holder
15 holes x 42 holes
Cut 2
Stitch front as graphed
Reverse back and stitch with
Reverse Continental Stitches,
omitting inner ears and face

COLOR KEY
DOG

Yards	Medium Weight Yarn
3 (2.8m)	■ Dark brown
1 (1m)	■ Black
10 (9.2m)	□ Pale yellow
	Uncoded areas are pale yellow Continental Stitches
	╱ Black Straight Stitch
	● Attach cabochon

COLOR KEY
CAT

Yards	Medium Weight Yarn
1 (1m)	■ Pink
10 (9.2m)	Uncoded areas are gold Continental Stitches
	╱ Gold Overcast and Whipstitch
1 (1m)	╱ Black Straight Stitch
	● Attach cabochon

Animal Foot
5 holes x 4 holes
Cut 4 each for
dog, cat, mouse and bear
Reverse 2
Stitch as graphed for dog
Replace pale yellow with gold for cat
Replace pale yellow with gray for mouse
Replace pale yellow with brown for bear

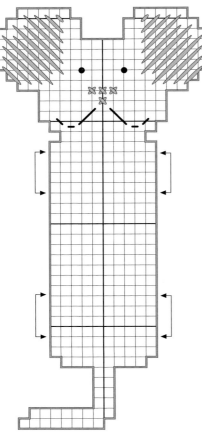

Frog Foot
5 holes x 3 holes
Cut 4, reverse 2

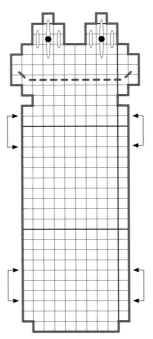

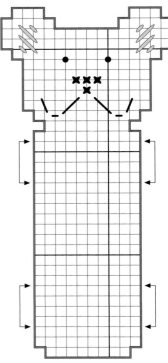

Mouse Treat Holder
20 holes x 41 holes
Cut 2
Stitch front as graphed
Reverse back and stitch with
Reverse Continental Stitches,
omitting inner ears and face

Frog Treat Holder
12 holes x 31 holes
Cut 2
Stitch front as graphed
Stitch back with green
Reverse Continental Stitches,
omitting face

Bear Treat Holder
16 holes x 34 holes
Cut 2
Stitch front as graphed
Stitch back with brown
Reverse Continental Stitches,
omitting inner ears and face

COLOR KEY
MOUSE

Yards	Medium Weight Yarn
1 (1m)	▨ Pink
11 (10.1m)	Uncoded areas are gray Continental Stitches
	╱ Gray Overcast and Whipstitch
1 (1m)	╱ Black Straight Stitch
	● Attach cabochon

COLOR KEY
FROG

Yards	Medium Weight Yarn
8 (7.4m)	■ Green
1 (1m)	☐ White
	Uncoded areas are green Continental Stitches
1 (1m)	╱ Red Backstitch
	● Attach cabochon

COLOR KEY
BEAR

Yards	Medium Weight Yarn
1 (1m)	☐ Tan
1 (1m)	■ Black
11 (10.1m)	Uncoded areas are brown Continental Stitches
	╱ Brown Overcast and Whipstitch
	╱ Black Straight Stitch
	● Attach cabochon

Tropical Fish Curtain Accents

Designs by Nanette M. Seale

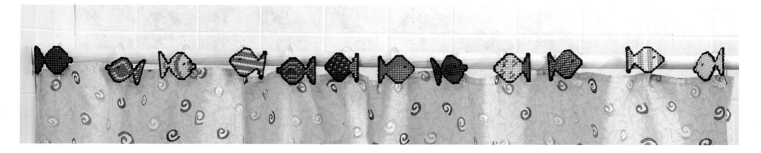

Size: Individual stitched fish vary from approximately 2 inches W x 2 inches H (5.1cm x 5.1cm) to 2⅜ inches W x 2 inches H (6cm x 5.1cm)

Skill Level: Beginner

Materials

One Set

❑ 1 sheet 7-count plastic canvas
❑ Plastic canvas yarn as listed in color key
❑ 12 clear plastic shower-curtain rings
❑ #16 tapestry needle
❑ Hot-glue gun

Stitching Step by Step

1 Cut plastic canvas according to graphs (page 29–31).

2 Stitch fish according to graphs, Overcasting with black.

3 Referring to photo, hot-glue fish to fronts of shower-curtain rings. (Closure of rings should be at bottom).

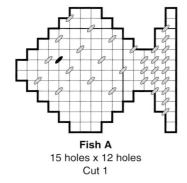

Fish A
15 holes x 12 holes
Cut 1

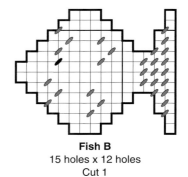

Fish B
15 holes x 12 holes
Cut 1

COLOR KEY

FISH A

Yards	Plastic Canvas Yarn
2 (1.9m)	■ Black
1 (1m)	▨ Lilac
2 (1.9m)	Uncoded areas are bright purple Continental Stitches

COLOR KEY

FISH B

Yards	Plastic Canvas Yarn
2 (1.9m)	■ Black
1 (1m)	▨ Red
2 (1.9m)	Uncoded areas are yellow Continental Stitches

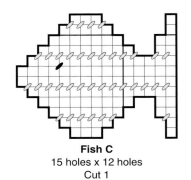

Fish C
15 holes x 12 holes
Cut 1

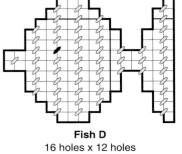

Fish D
16 holes x 12 holes
Cut 1

COLOR KEY
FISH C

Yards	Plastic Canvas Yarn
2 (1.9m)	■ Black
1 (1m)	☐ Bright yellow-green
1 (1m)	Uncoded areas are bright pink Continental Stitches

COLOR KEY
FISH D

Yards	Plastic Canvas Yarn
2 (1.9m)	■ Black
1 (1m)	☐ Bright yellow-green
1 (1m)	Uncoded areas are light green Continental Stitches

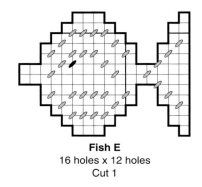

Fish E
16 holes x 12 holes
Cut 1

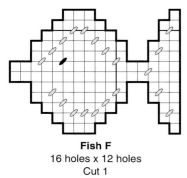

Fish F
16 holes x 12 holes
Cut 1

COLOR KEY
FISH E

Yards	Plastic Canvas Yarn
2 (1.9m)	■ Black
1 (1m)	▨ Orange
1 (1m)	Uncoded areas are royal blue Continental Stitches

COLOR KEY
FISH F

Yards	Plastic Canvas Yarn
2 (1.9m)	■ Black
1 (1m)	☐ Bright yellow-green
2 (1.9m)	Uncoded areas are rose Continental Stitches

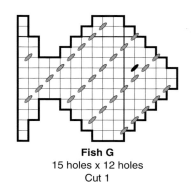

Fish G
15 holes x 12 holes
Cut 1

COLOR KEY
FISH G

Yards	Plastic Canvas Yarn
2 (1.9m)	■ Black
1 (1m)	▨ Burnt orange
2 (1.9m)	Uncoded areas are parrot green Continental Stitches

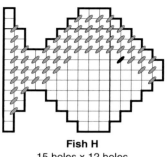

Fish H
15 holes x 12 holes
Cut 1

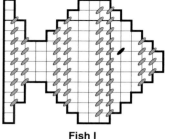

Fish I
15 holes x 12 holes
Cut 1

COLOR KEY
FISH H
Yards	Plastic Canvas Yarn
2 (1.9m)	■ Black
1 (1m)	▨ Bright pink
1 (1m)	Uncoded areas are blue Continental Stitches

COLOR KEY
FISH I
Yards	Plastic Canvas Yarn
2 (1.9m)	■ Black
1 (1m)	▨ Orange
1 (1m)	Uncoded areas are lime Continental Stitches

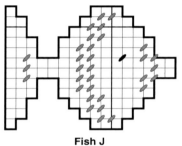

Fish J
16 holes x 12 holes
Cut 1

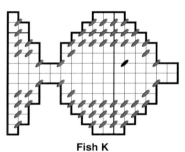

Fish K
16 holes x 12 holes
Cut 1

COLOR KEY
FISH J
Yards	Plastic Canvas Yarn
2 (1.9m)	■ Black
1 (1m)	▨ Blue
2 (1.9m)	Uncoded areas are bright yellow-green Continental Stitches

COLOR KEY
FISH K
Yards	Plastic Canvas Yarn
2 (1.9m)	■ Black
1 (1m)	▨ Red
1 (1m)	Uncoded areas are royal blue Continental Stitches

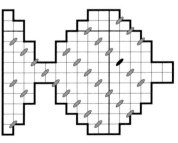

Fish L
16 holes x 12 holes
Cut 1

COLOR KEY
FISH L
Yards	Plastic Canvas Yarn
2 (1.9m)	■ Black
1 (1m)	▨ Teal
2 (1.9m)	Uncoded areas are bright purple Continental Stitches

The full line of The Needlecraft Shop
products is carried by Annie's Attic catalog.
TOLL-FREE ORDER LINE
or to request a free catalog
(800) 582-6643
Customer Service
(800) 449-0440
Fax (800) 882-6643
Visit AnniesAttic.com

ISBN: 978-1-57367-301-3

Printed in USA

2 3 4 5 6 7 8 9

Shopping for Supplies

For supplies, first shop your local craft
and needlework stores. Some supplies
may be found in fabric, hardware and
discount stores. If you are unable to find
the supplies you need, please call Annie's
Attic at (800) 259-4000 to request a free
catalog that sells plastic canvas supplies.

Getting Started

Before You Cut

Buy one brand of canvas for each entire project, as brands can differ slightly in the distance between bars. Count holes carefully from the graph before you cut, using the bolder lines that show each 10 holes. These 10-mesh lines begin in the lower left corner of each graph to make counting easier. Mark canvas before cutting, then remove all marks completely before stitching. If the piece is cut in a rectangular or square shape and is either not worked, or worked with only one color and one type of stitch, the graph is not included in the pattern. Instead, the cutting and stitching instructions are given in the general instructions or with the individual project instructions.

Covering the Canvas

Bring needle up from back of work, leaving a short length of yarn on back of canvas; work over short length to secure. To end a thread, weave needle and thread through the wrong side of your last few stitches; clip. Follow the numbers on the small graphs beside each stitch illustration; bring your needle up from the back of the work on odd numbers and down through the front of the work on even numbers. Work embroidery stitches last, after the canvas has been completely covered by the needlepoint stitches.

Basic Stitches

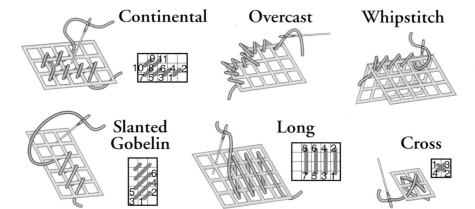

Embroidery Stitches

French Knot

Lazy Daisy

Backstitch

Straight

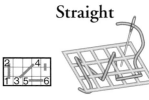

METRIC KEY:
millimeters = (mm)
centimeters = (cm)
meters = (m)
grams = (g)

ISBN: 978-1-57367-301-3

U.S. $7.95

0 54525 22014 6

PRINTED IN USA
DRGnetwork.com

THE BULLS

A season to remember